Those who helped.

Allan, for his encouragement, Glynis for her good-humoured assistance, Gerry and Thingie, and friends too numerous to name who have put up with the author apparently talking to himself these last few months. Most important of all Terry, best friend and superwife without whom this book would not have been written. To all these people, Rhoofus and I say

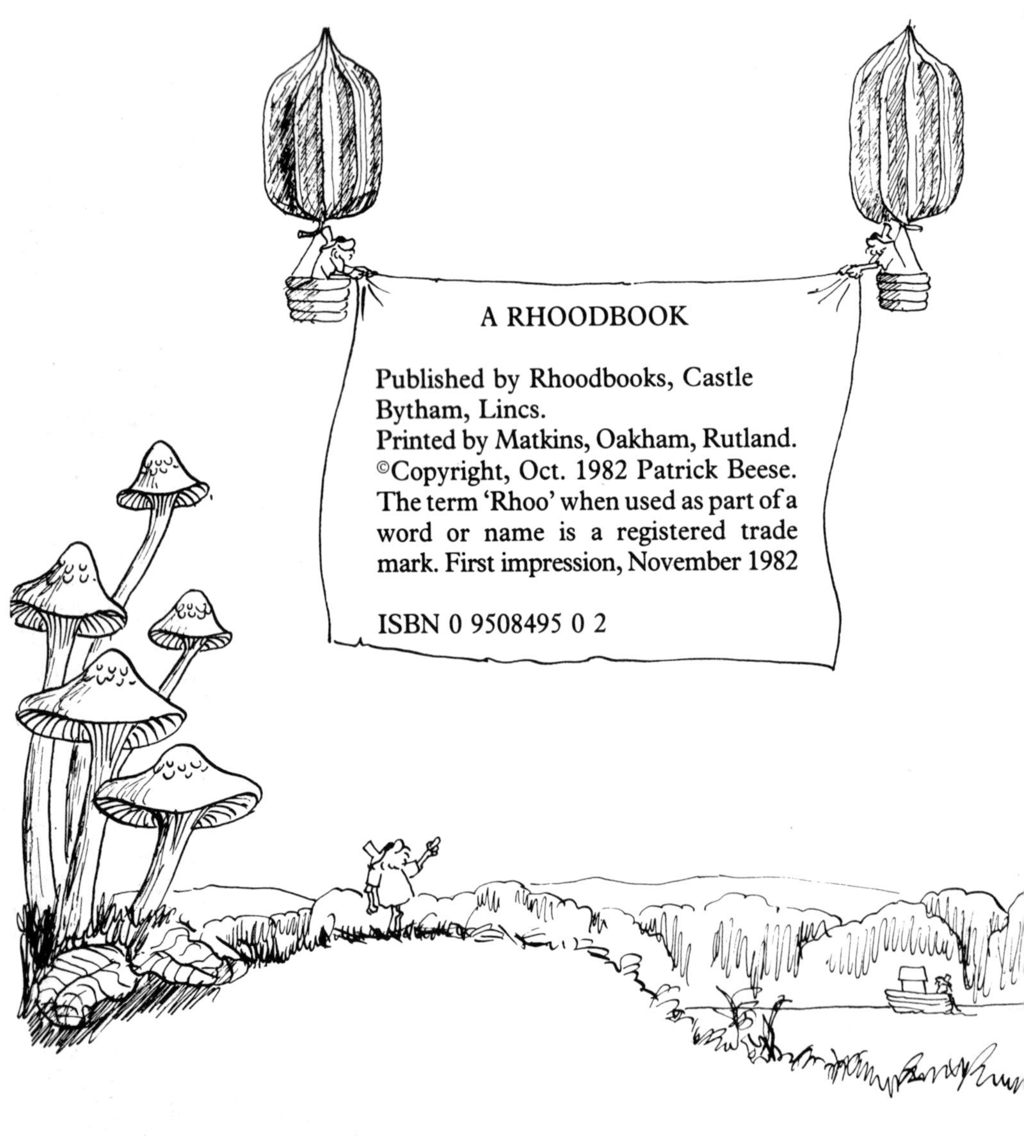

A RHOODBOOK

Published by Rhoodbooks, Castle Bytham, Lincs.
Printed by Matkins, Oakham, Rutland.

First impression, November 1982

ISBN 0 9508495 0 2

The Rhoodmen of Rutland
written and illustrated
by
Patrick Beese

The Rhoodmen of Rutland are an ancient race of small people who live on, and around, the great lake known as:

Rutland

Water,

down in deepest Rutland. The Rhoodmen have lived, and thrived there since the end of the last ice age, when the lake was first formed.

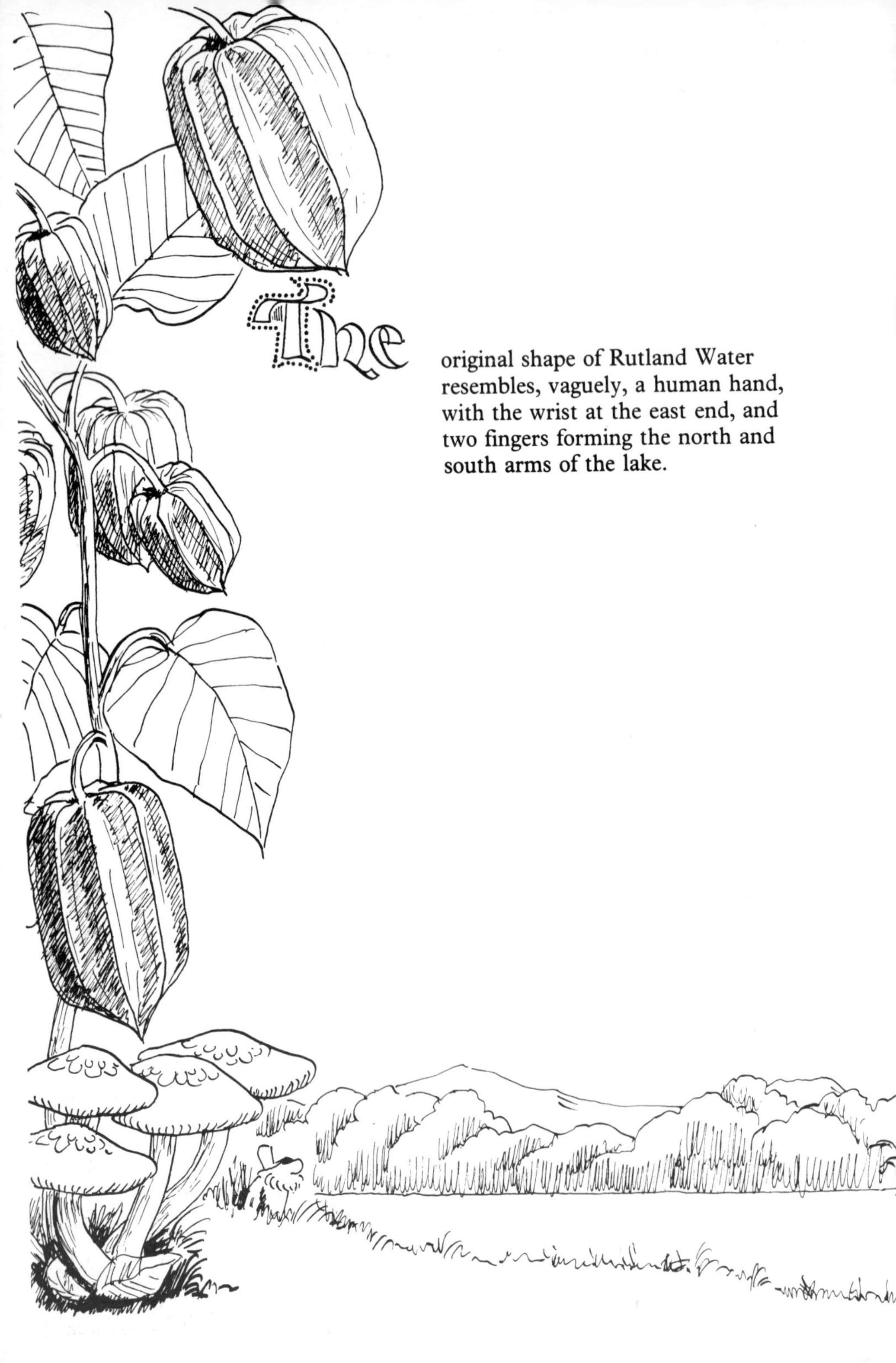

The original shape of Rutland Water resembles, vaguely, a human hand, with the wrist at the east end, and two fingers forming the north and south arms of the lake.

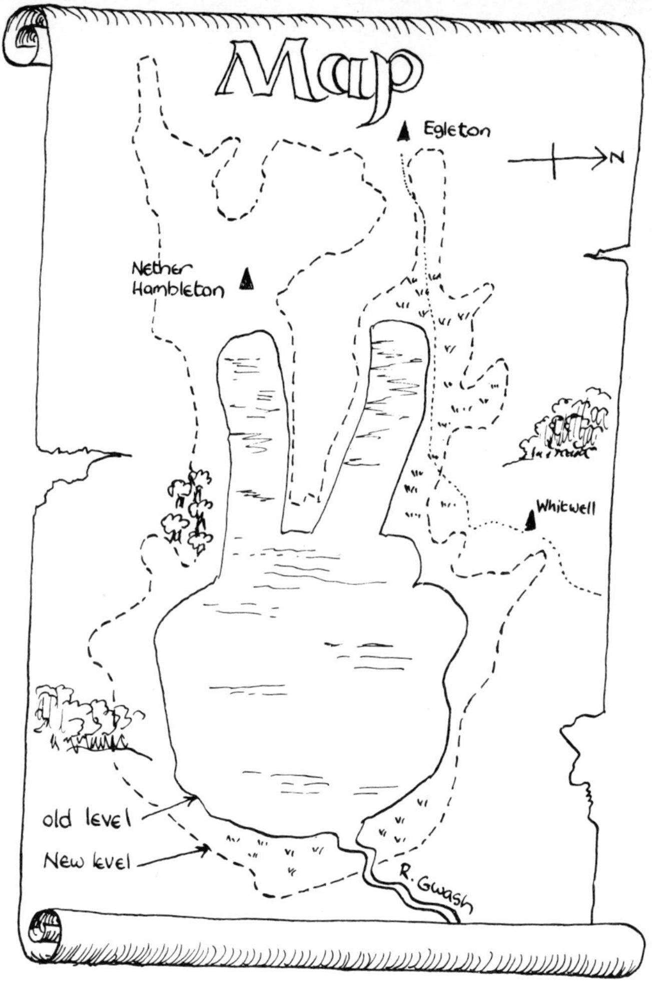

Map

Egleton
N
Nether Hambleton
Whitwell
old level
New level
R. Gwash

The shape of the lake was changed somewhat when the Anglian Water Authority raised the level by building a dam at the east end across the course of the River Gwash, effectively inundating the settlement at Nether Hambleton, an act which particularly annoyed the Rhoodmen.

of the information for this work came from two sources. The important archaeological evidence came from excavations made at the site of the old Rhoodic settlement at Nether Hambleton. We were able to record the rhoonic inscriptions on the Great Rhood Stone and, from it, deduce much about the old ways of the Rhood Folk. This valuable site has since disappeared with the raising of the lake level.

Contemporary evidence of their way of life came from personal contact with some of the present generation of Rhoodmen, in particular...

Rhoofus,

who we found, or, to be more accurate,
who found us, down by the waters
side one quiet evening, around sunset.

We were walking from Egleton to Whitwell that evening. The sun was slowly sinking over Brooke Hill lighting the tops of the trees with a beautiful golden colour. We sat down to rest and watch the evening pageant of nature's hues.
It was very peaceful.

Abruptly we realised we were not quite alone. Standing watching us from a nearby rock was a small man, about 9 inches tall, with a bushy white beard and a rather long nose. He was wearing a rough brown smock, woven, we thought from animal hair, and a tall hat made from the same material. He eyed us steadily for several moments before speaking.

“You realise,” he said, “that it’s going to take quite some time to clear up the mess you’ve made!”

We looked around but couldn’t see a thing out of place. Apologizing somewhat, we pointed this out.

“At least two of my friends will have to move house on account of your clumsy feet” he said, and pointed to a toadstool, now shattered, a few feet away. Sure enough it had small windows and doors intricately built into it. A chimney pot stuck out of the top and a tiny verandah with a rail around it completed the job. It was now a sorry sight. “I don’t know what I’ll tell them when they get back,” he complained. We asked if we could do anything to help.

“Well, if you people would understand more about what goes on around here it might do some good, ” he said. “Humans don’t seem to be able to go anywhere without breaking or spoiling something on the way.”

....we decided there and then to dedicate ourselves to informing and educating the human race in the ways of these folk. The little man agreed.

"Let's begin now!" he exclaimed, and, bowing low he introduced himself. "My name," he said, "is Rhoofus, and I am one of the

Come here every evening and I will tell you all about us. But," he warned us, "Don't bring anyone else with you and be careful where you put your feet next time."

And he was gone.

Next evening we returned with pencil and drawing pad. We had, instinctively left the camera at home. We subsequently managed to photograph Rhoofus in one of his unguarded moments but when we developed the film there was not a trace of him on the negative, a fact which still remains unexplained. Rhoofus appeared as quietly before and we sat down to listen to him.

He talked and we listened, taking copious notes and many drawings. Occasionally he would stop for a few moments to correct the spelling of a word here or a drawing there.

And he told us about Rhoodmen and their way of life. About their houses made in the giant toadstools found only in Rutland, and about the summer houseboats made of woven waterweed. About the mysterious leylines which cause the breeze to blow and which can be used to power the weed houseboats. About Rhood cuisine and the delicacies to be found in the woods and hedgerows. About Rhood language and literature, recorded in Rhoonic on weed-made paper: He talked and talked holding us spellbound.

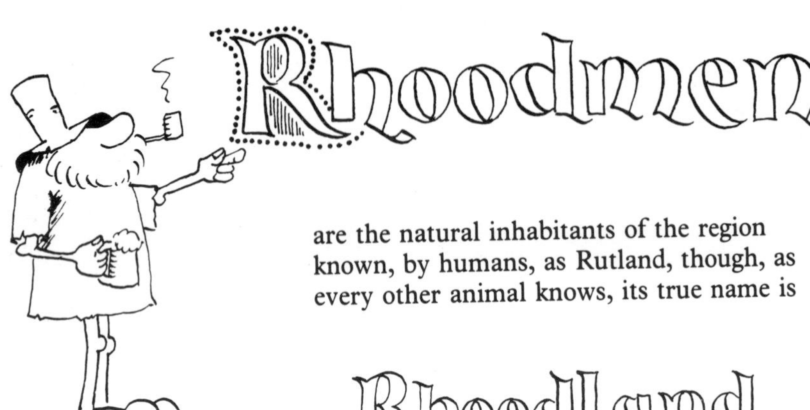

Rhoodmen

are the natural inhabitants of the region known, by humans, as Rutland, though, as every other animal knows, its true name is

Rhoodland

Their origins start fairly early on in the evolutionary chain.

The evidence

for the now well-established fact that Rhoodmen are significantly more intelligent than modern man comes from the discovery, at Empingham, of a rhood skull, some 30,000 years old, found during excavations for the new dam.

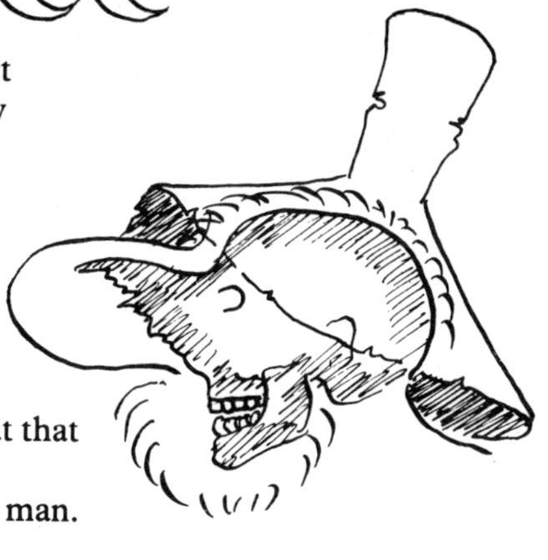

This skull shows that even at that time, Homo Rhoodus had a proportionally larger brain than man.

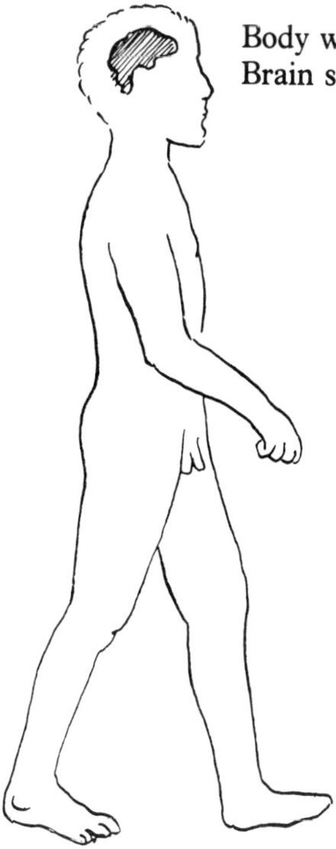

Body weight — 140 lb.
Brain size — 4 lb
Ratio, 35 to 1

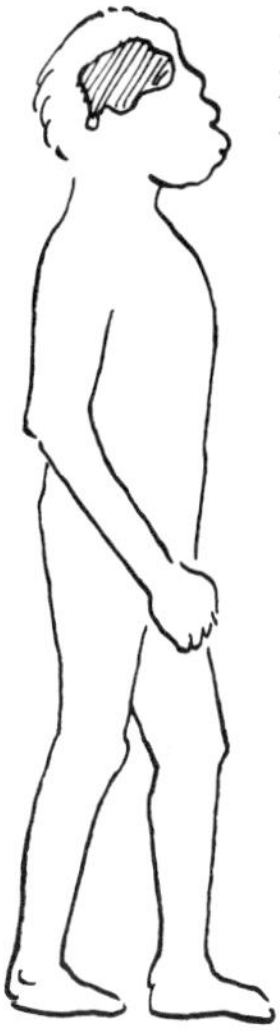

Body weight — 80 lb
Brain size — 3.2 lb
Ratio, 25 to 1

Body weight — 20 lb
Brain size — 2 lb
Ratio, 10 to 1

Homo Sapiens

Australopithicus

Homo Rhoodus

The

Qualities

of Rhoodmen are not strained! Rhoodmen have most of the good points which humans would like to have. They are...

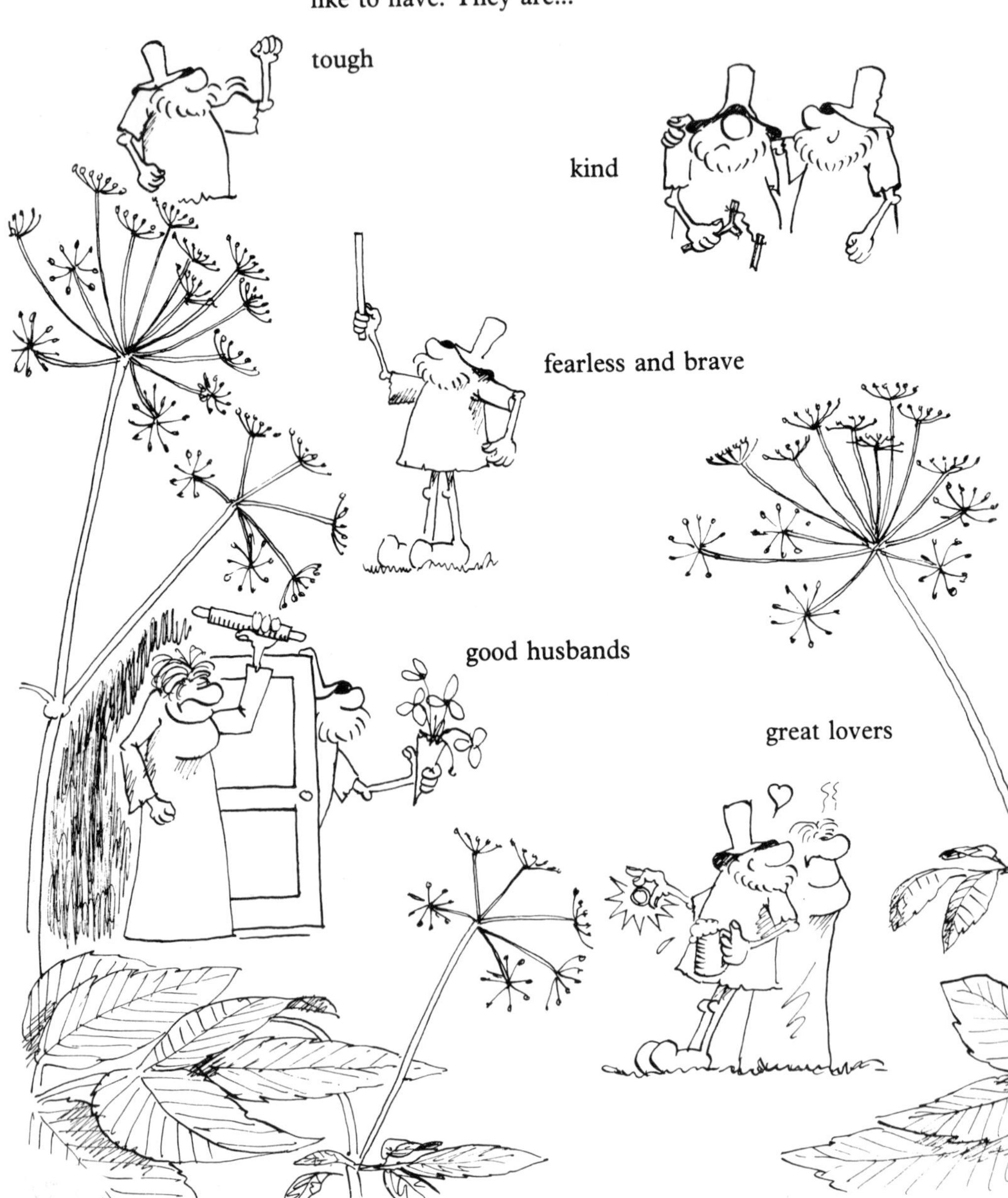

when the occasion demands it they can be

downright lazy!

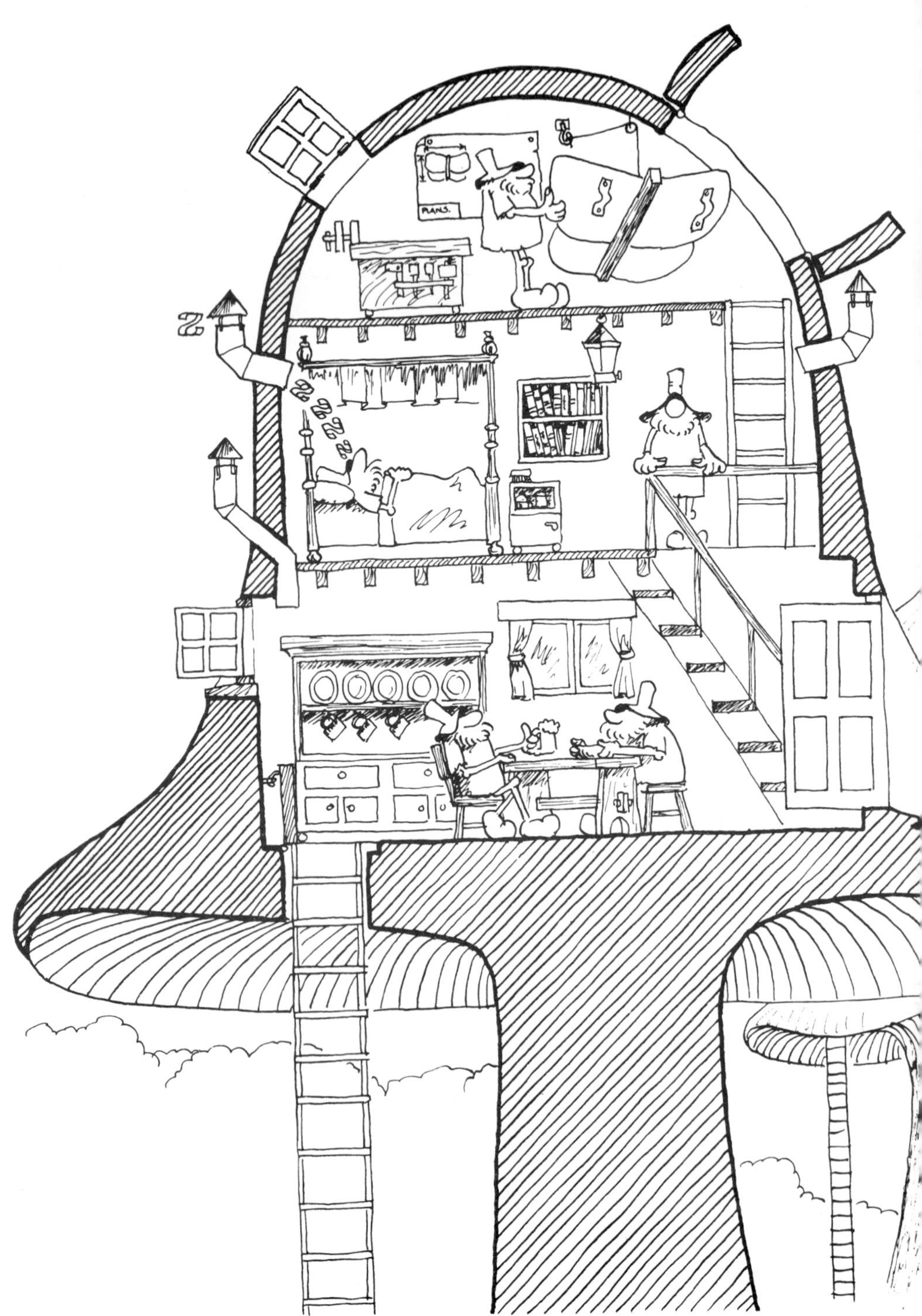
PLANS.

Rhoodhomes

Rhoodmen make their houses in hollowed-out giant toadstools; found only in Rutland and known, botanically, as Agaricus Rhoodus Maximus. Considerable ingenuity is put into the building and layout of a rhoodhouse with the main living rooms on the bottom layer, the sleeping quarters on the next, and the workshops and studios at the top.

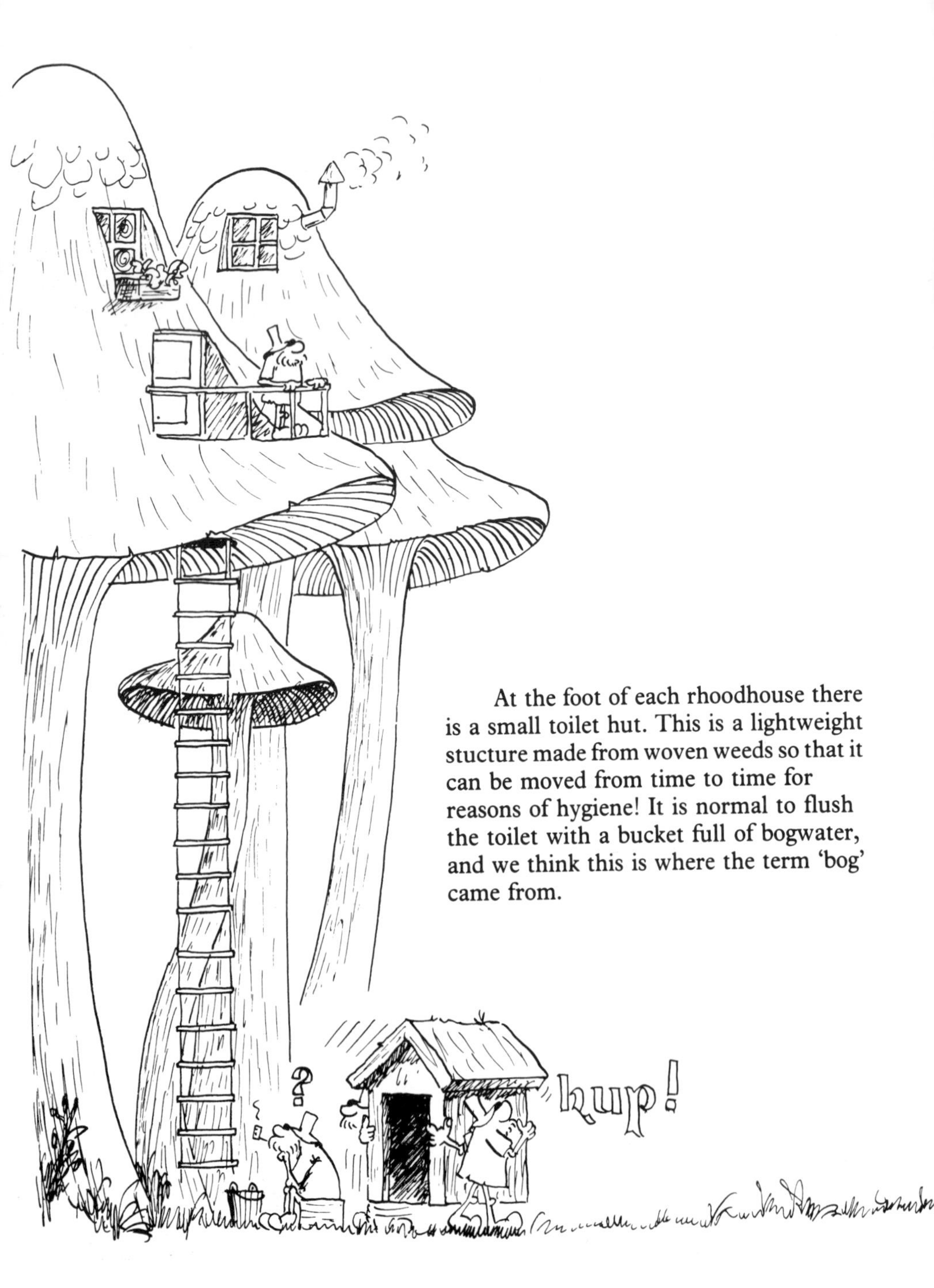

At the foot of each rhoodhouse there is a small toilet hut. This is a lightweight stucture made from woven weeds so that it can be moved from time to time for reasons of hygiene! It is normal to flush the toilet with a bucket full of bogwater, and we think this is where the term 'bog' came from.

Since the Rhoodmen won't have anything to do with science they haven't worked out why some toadstools grow faster than others!

The Rhoodmen are, of course, excellent

boatbuilders

and amongst their many aquatic accomplishments are

the woven-weed raft, for short journeys in sheltered waters, though they can have disadvantages at times...

...something a little more ambitious for fishing expeditions...

...while most Rhoodmen have a houseboat for a summer residence.

All these craft are made from twisted 'ropes' of dried water weed pleated into solid hanks which are stitched together.

The resultant hull has inherent flotation from the tightly packed weed, and the earliest designs almost certainly pre-date the Egyptian papyrus boats.

To make a weedboat...

...first a frame of branches is formed starting with the keel which is bent, to shape, over a convenient rock...

...and held down by convenient Rhoodmen.

Repeat the process for the side frames.

Meanwhile dried weed
is twisted into rope...
...by keeping a good
hold of the end.
A little lubrication
sometimes helps!

Then tie the rope to the frame, removing the Rhoodmen in sequence.
'seems a pity to wake the 'guv!
zzzz
Lash together larger twists of rope to form an impermeable mat for the hull. Last of all don't forget to remove the rock before rolling upside down...
zzzz

and launching, making sure, of course,

that the future owner has a ringside view!

Still, when all's done and fitted out the weed-houseboat is a Rhoodman's summer home, an essay in rhood craftsmanship and skill.

The pride and joy of the Rhood fleet are the long distance

which come in a variety of shapes, sizes and designs, the most ambitious being the large galleon-like, boats used for exploring the far-flung corners of Rutland Water. Their motive power is, believe it or not, stones!

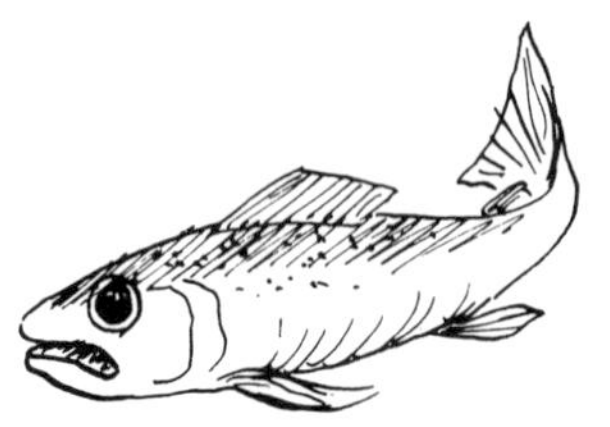

Special stones, called leystones are, or rather were, collected from around the Great Rhoodstone at Nether Hambleton, and placed in line along the keel of the boat. These have the effect of drawing the boat along the ancient leylines which criss-cross Rutland.

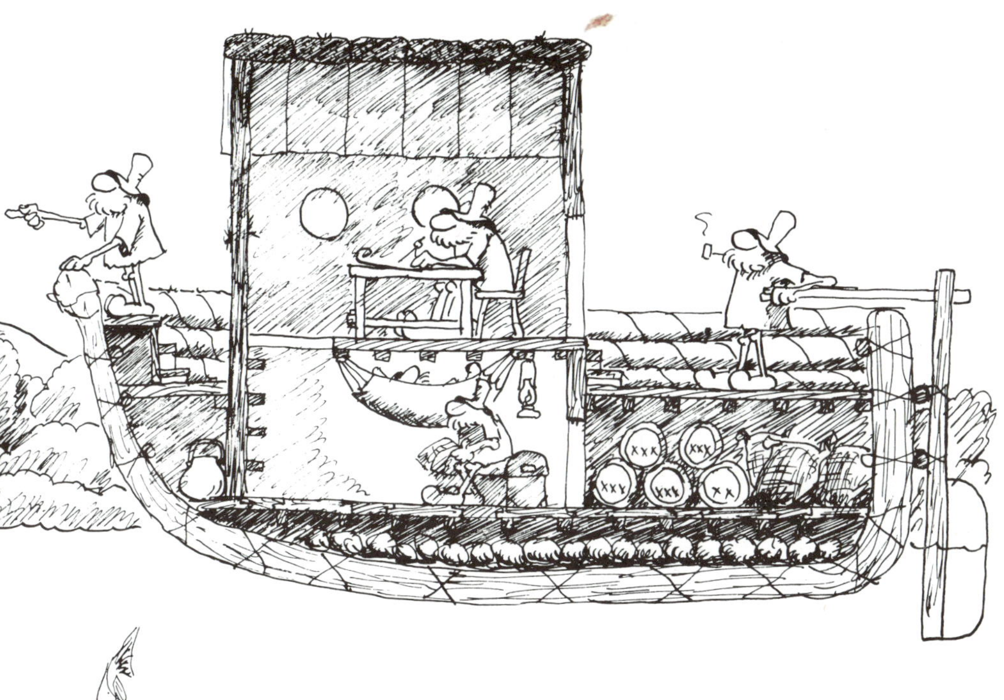

While the stones are in place the boat will drift along a convenient leyline at about four human knots. To stop the boat simply remove the middle stone, and to return the same way just simply re-arrange the stones in reverse order.

Leylines

exist all over Rutland. They are straight lines of magnetic force, acting in a horizontal direction, and radiating out from the Great Rhood Stone. A great deal of superstition surrounds this stone. Some Rhoodmen think that it is the petrified remains of the Great God, Rhoo, who came down to Rhoodland (Rutland) at the dawn of time before the Ice Ages, who made war on the Gods of the Sun and the Moon, was overwhelmed by their strength and frozen into rock as a punishment. These same Rhoodmen also think that the sound of the wind on stormy nights is the call of the Wind God, trying to free Rhoo from his imprisonment. On such nights they will hide under their beds and stay there till dawn.

Such fears are, of course, ridiculous!

Be that as it may the leylines coming from the Great Rhood Stone are put to good use by the Rhoodmen, not only as power for the boats but also as direction finders. In one sense they are as good as modern radar. Let us explain.

In addition to the main leylines from the Great Rhood Stone there are also secondary leylines which cut across them at varying angles. Where they intersect they form a clockwise turning force! This turning force is used by the boats rather like a roundabout. There is usually a marker with a position code flag on it, rotating gently in the middle.

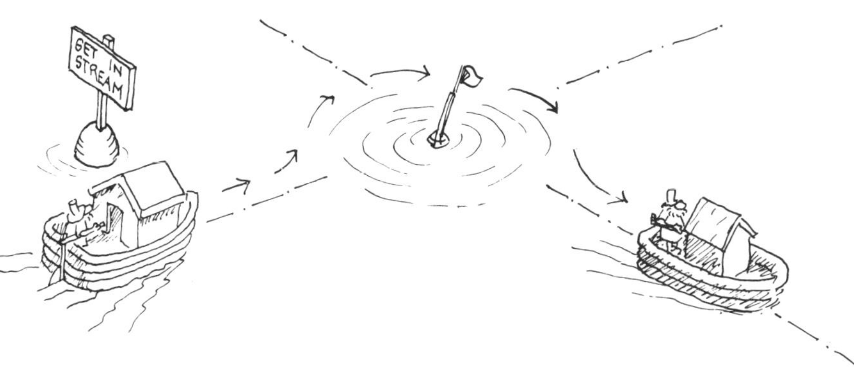

land leylines are useful for finding one's position and in charting maps for other travellers. For this you need a leyline hanging stone — a small piece of leystone tied to a short length of string.

If the stone does nothing (i.e. just hangs) then you are not on a leyline.

On the other hand if the stone assumes one position and always returns to it, even when moved then you are on a leyline.

If, however, the stone spins slowly and continuously clockwise then you are on a leyline junction.

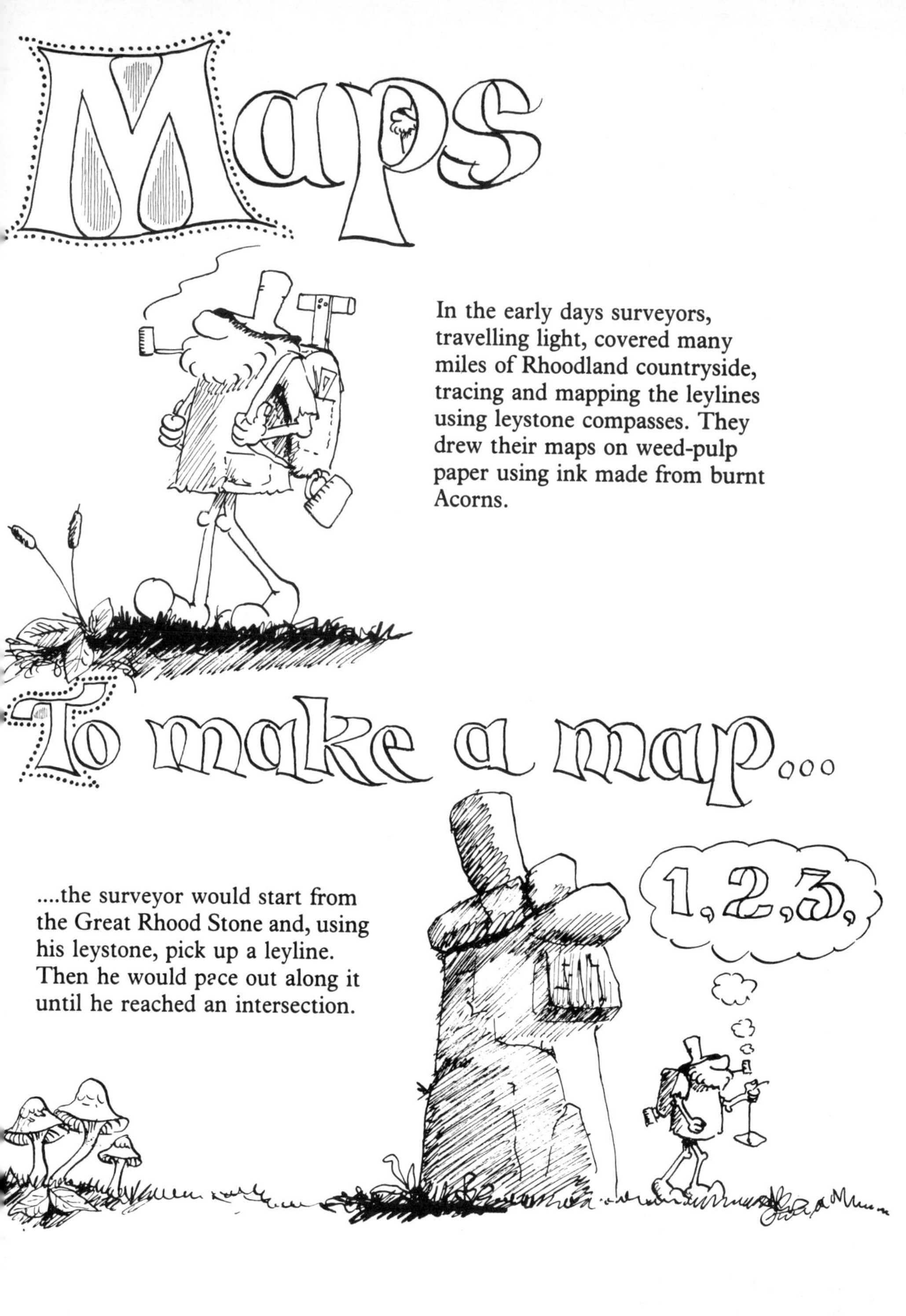

Maps

In the early days surveyors, travelling light, covered many miles of Rhoodland countryside, tracing and mapping the leylines using leystone compasses. They drew their maps on weed-pulp paper using ink made from burnt Acorns.

To make a map...

....the surveyor would start from the Great Rhood Stone and, using his leystone, pick up a leyline. Then he would pace out along it until he reached an intersection.

the stone started spinning a stick was placed and a code marked on it which was then transferred to the map.

Intersections were coded by putting a major leyline number in front of a minor one, and then classified as left and right, depending on how they faced the Great Rhood Stone.

Here is a fragment of an early leychart found near Whitwell.

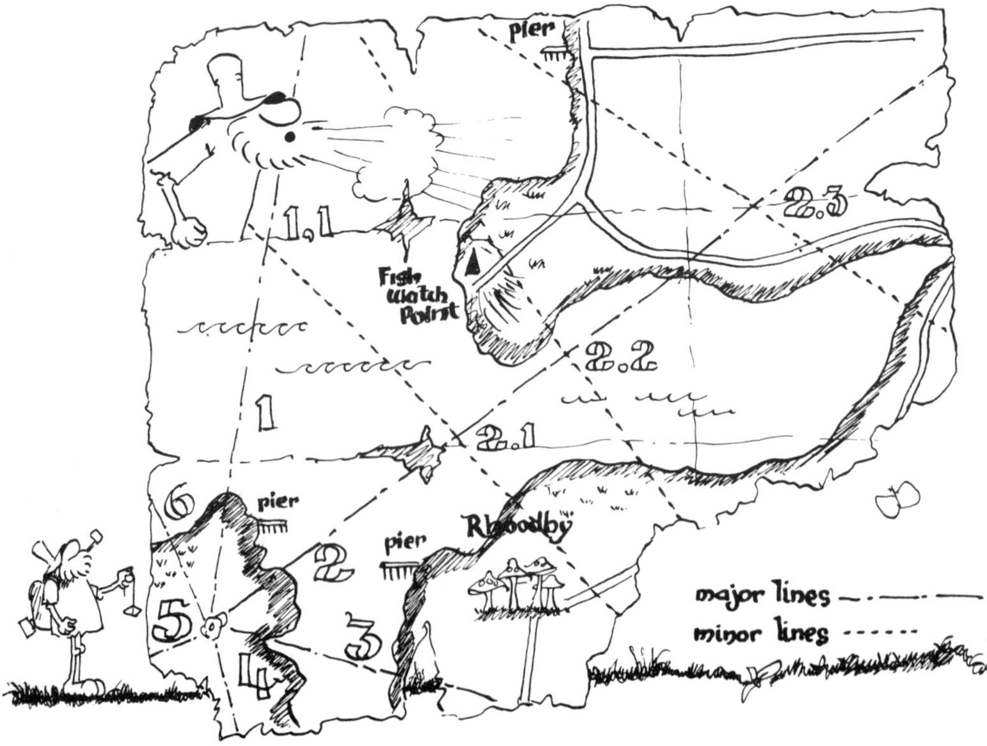

Mind you, even with a map some Rhoodmen can get lost, a characteristic which they share with most humans.

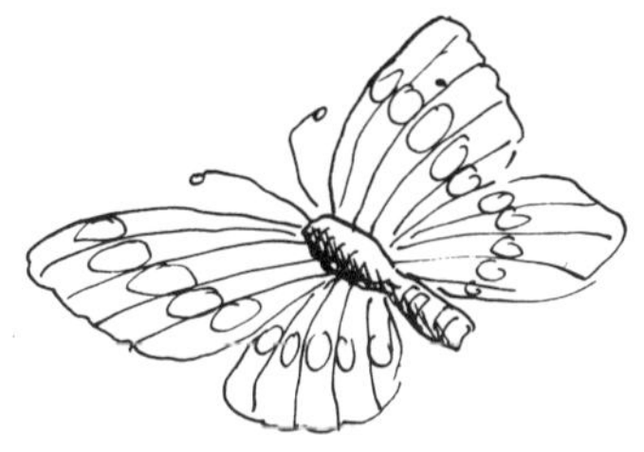

Wind power

In Rhoodland the wind is used as a major source of renewable energy. Giant sycamore seeds are used as vanes and hazel nuts are used as cams so that when the shaft turns the cam raises and lowers a beam.

Paper is made from weed pulp using wind power. The beam is used to pound weed stalks into pulp by adding water to the already pounded stalks. The pulp is collected and then poured into a large stone vat. Starch from boiled weed seed is added as a binder.

The mixture is stirred and then scooped up into a shallow wooden frame with a skin of muslin-like material made from woven spiders web. This is called a deckle. The surplus water is allowed to drain through the muslin and the sheet of damp paper is then tipped out onto a flat rock on which has been laid thin threads (these form the lines on the paper.) Finally the sheets are pegged out to dry.

In spite of all this
apparent activity the

of life, in Rhoodland is
relatively slow.

I think I
slept on an
acorn

Hey! What
happened to
you?

Weed farming

is a highly

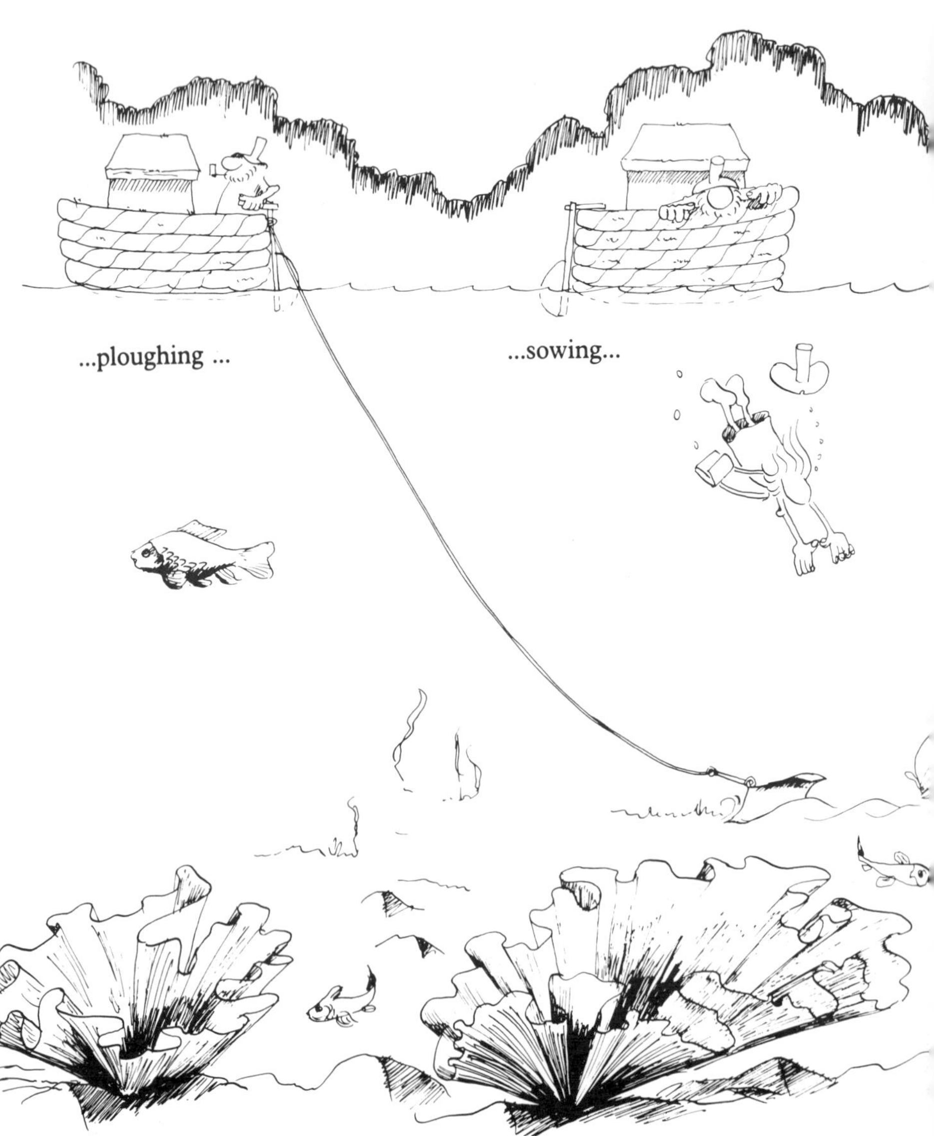

specialised profession. Each stage in weed cultivation is carefully worked on, with the latest equipment for....

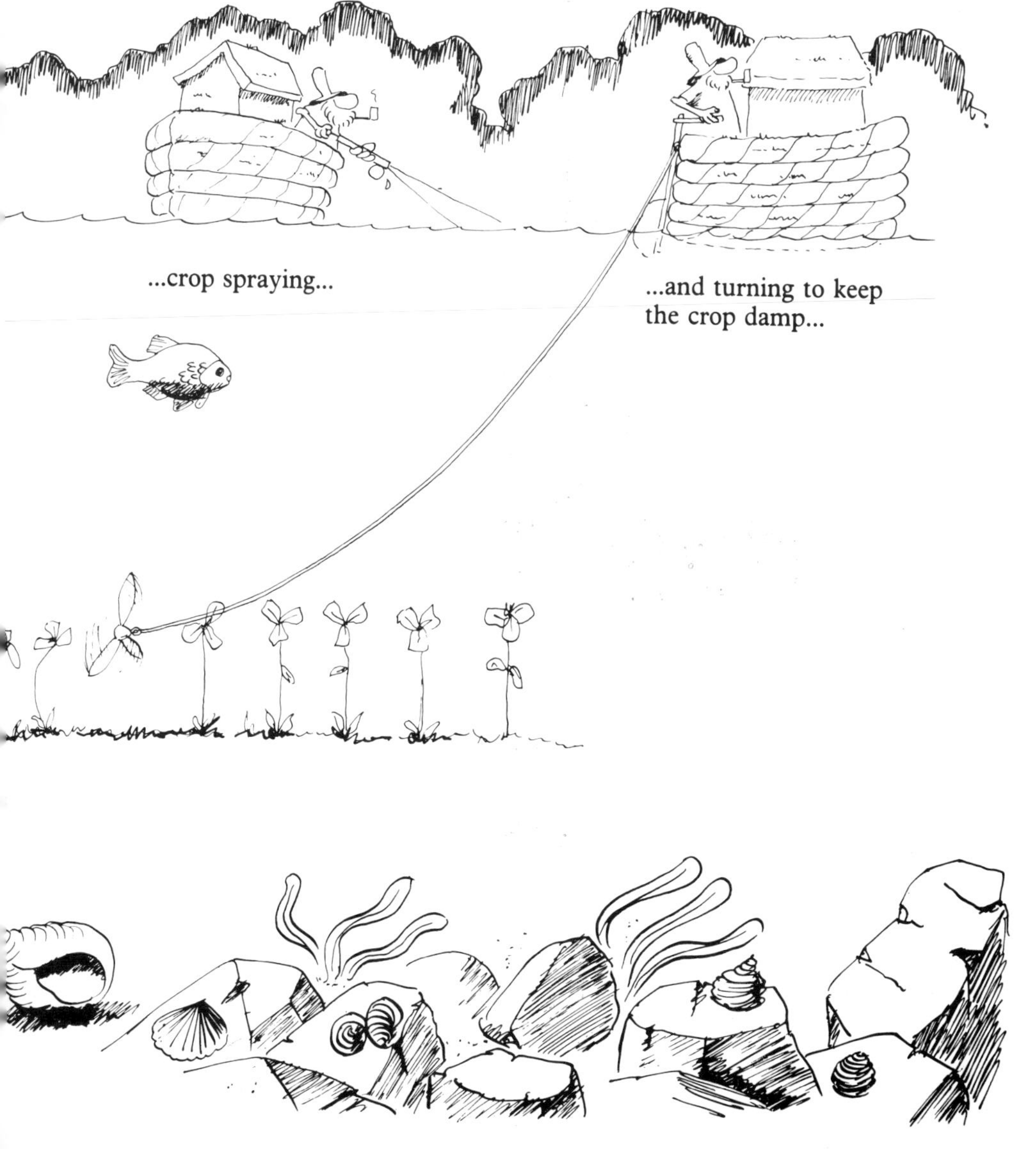

...crop spraying...

...and turning to keep the crop damp...

Harvesting

is usually done in pairs by trawling with a fork and basket.

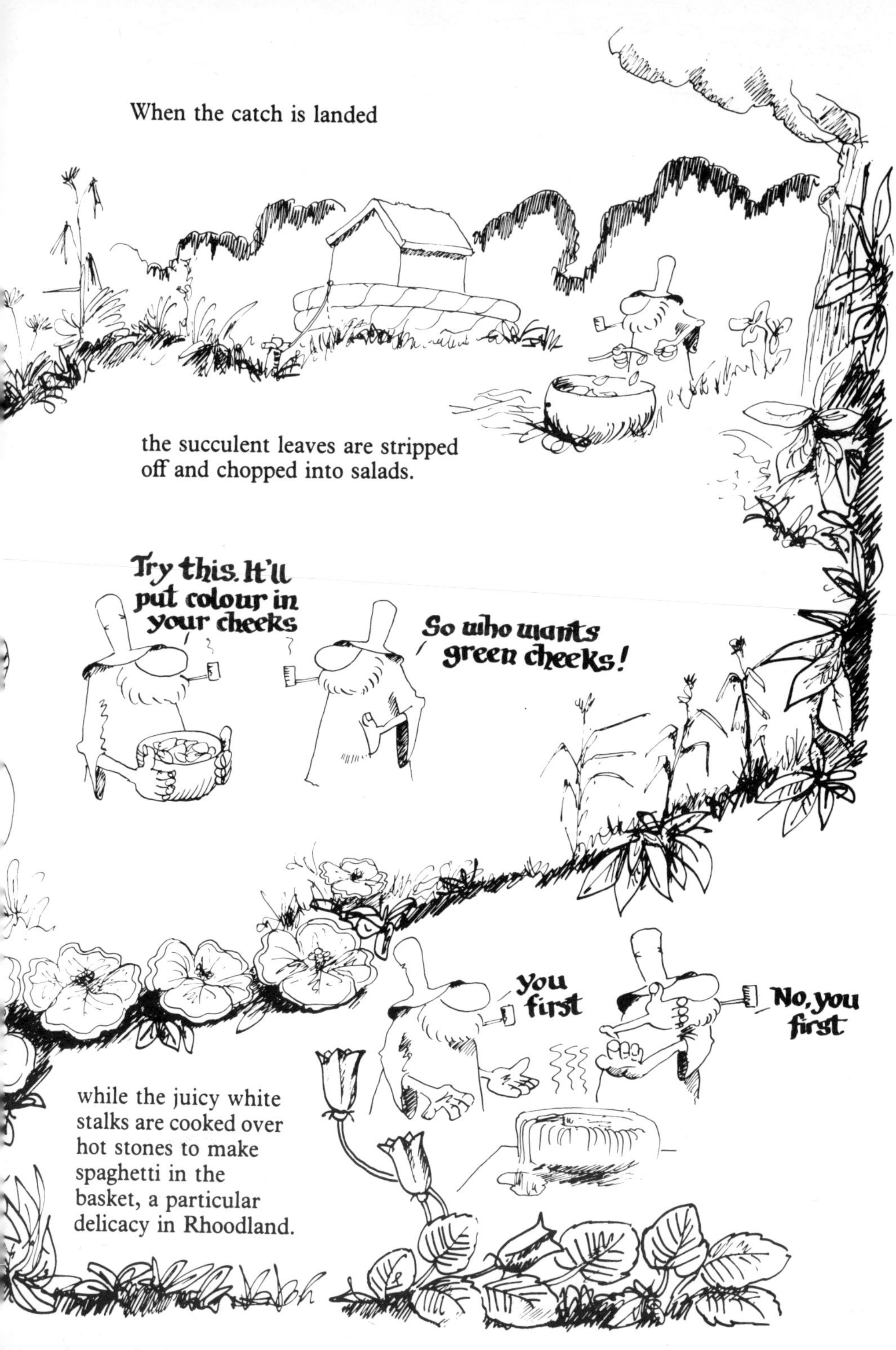
When the catch is landed
the succulent leaves are stripped off and chopped into salads.
Try this. It'll put colour in your cheeks
So who wants green cheeks!
You first
No, you first
while the juicy white stalks are cooked over hot stones to make spaghetti in the basket, a particular delicacy in Rhoodland.

The Annual
Weed show
Prize growths are
jealously guarded...
...and given extra special attention.

The winner receives much acclaim...

...and the winning weed is suitably decorated.

Fish

The Rhoodmen's favourite fish is the Pollack, a relative of the cod. They are highly praised by Rhood gourmets...

...especially when smoked.

To catch pollack the Rhoodmen hunt in fleets. The fish are known to swim in compact shoals, so one Rhoodman usually stands watch on a high piece of land overlooking the water, searching for the tell-tale signs of the shoal. The others while away the long idle hours...

...sometimes playing stone bowls to pass the time.

Suddenly the watcher stiffens, alert. He shades his eyes and stares. Yes! The well-known signs are spotted. He rouses the waiting Rhoodmen with the traditional cry of...

Pollocks!

...and the Rhoodmen scramble for their boats!

Of course, boats are not just used for fishing. However, the use of boats as modules in Rhoodlands form of high-rise housing is a relatively recent invention.

It was the habit for Rhoodmen to lie out on the roofs of their houseboats as they drifted in the sun, so as to be able to keep an eye on things and make sure that they were not drifting into anything too solid. To call it navigation is to give it too grand a title.

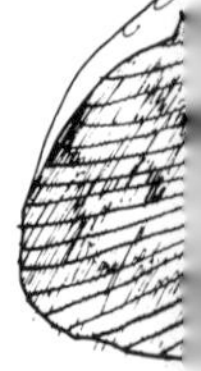

Which is all right as long as the sun shines.
Unfortunately one day...

The rains came

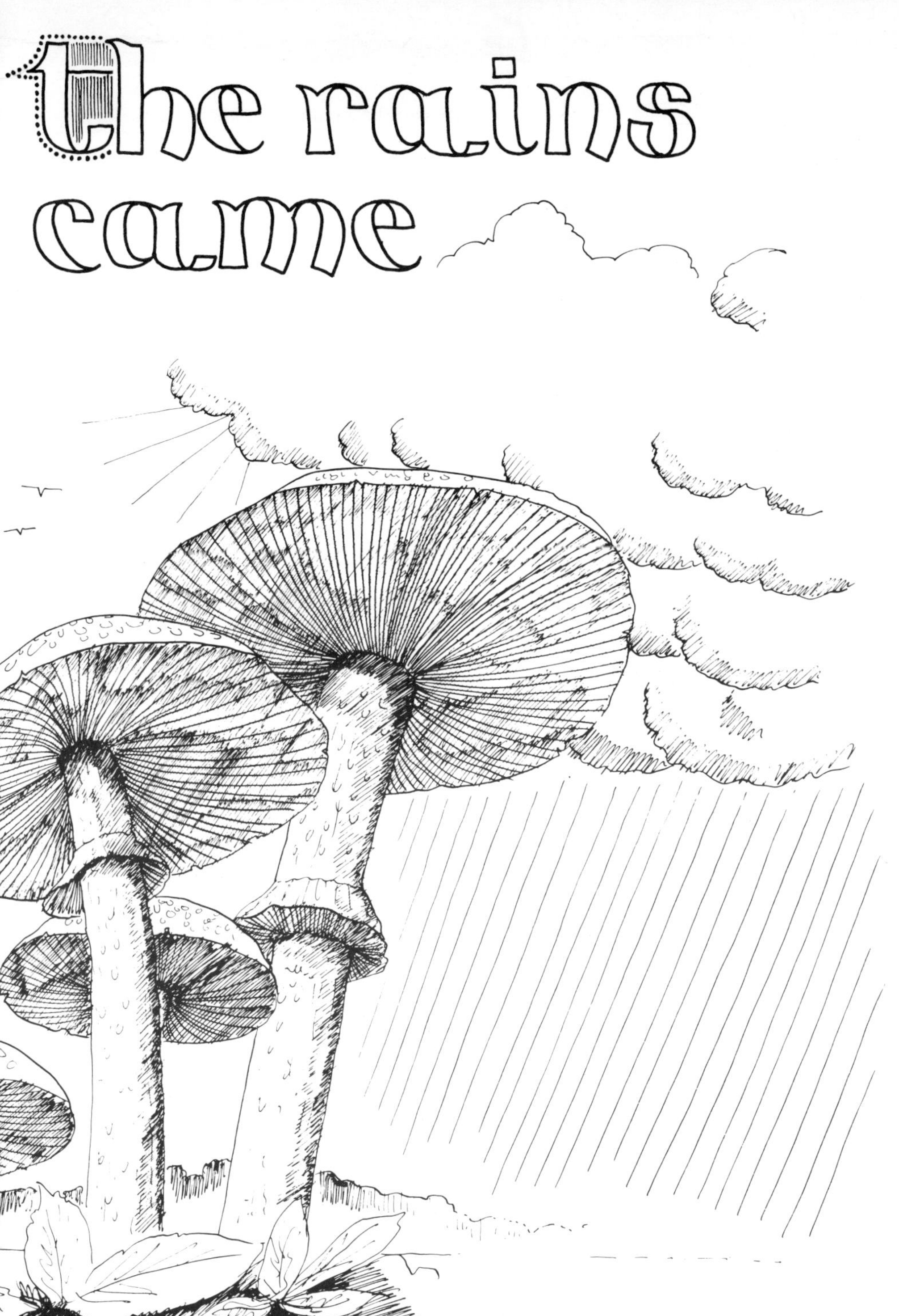

The rain came down,
the waters rose, and
the Rhoodmen drifted.

To stop their boats from drifting aimlessly some Rhoodmen drove long branches into the mud, two on each side, and tied their weedboats to them. Then they went below to get out of the rain.

While the Rhoodmen slept the rain stopped, the sun came out...

...and the waters fell, leaving the weedboats hanging in the air.

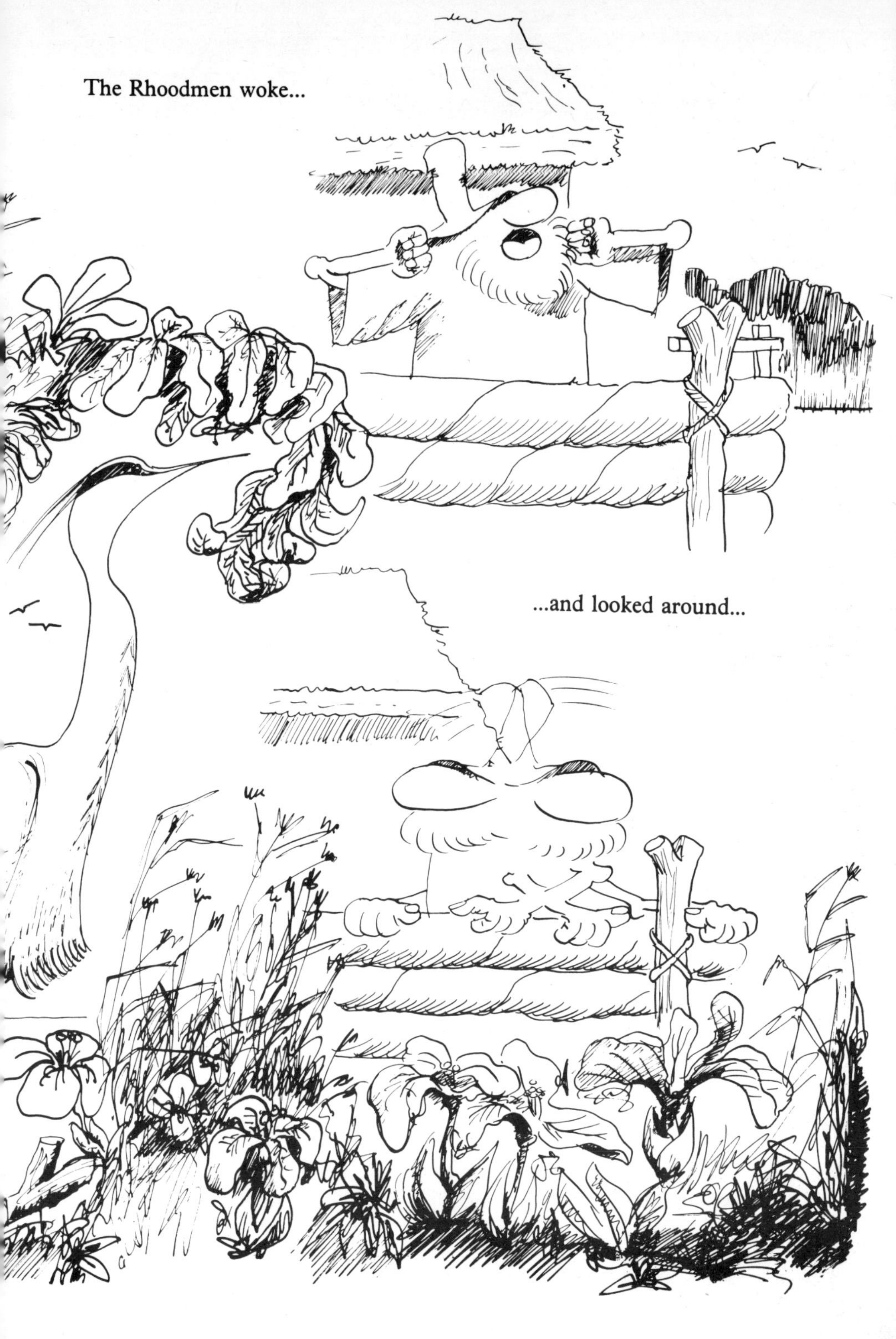
The Rhoodmen woke...
...and looked around...

...and found themselves high and dry.

All except one Rhoodman who hadn't tied his boat to branches and was still drifting about, accidentally under one of the stranded, hanging weedboats.

The two Rhoodmen came to an agreement...

....and a rope ladder was found

The two Rhoodmen became firm friends, and decided to tie their boats together permanently. At the next flood they allowed their boats to rise with the water, so that the bottom boat didn't flood, and then they tied the pair off at the height of the floodwater. Thus, when the water level dropped there was room underneath for yet another boat. And so on. In this way tall houseboats, with many levels became popular because you didn't need to take a boat to visit a friend. You just went upstairs.

At about this time parties became correspondingly more popular, and the rise to fame of Rhoodland ale dates from around this time.

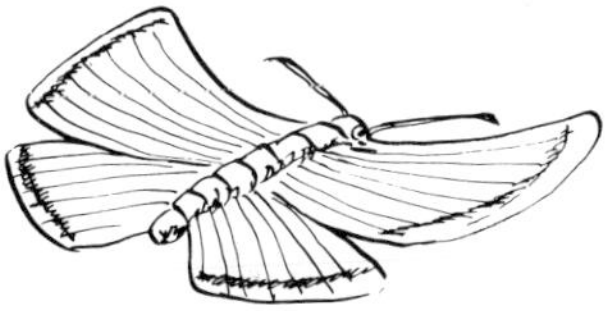

In Rhoodland today the high summer is regarded as a time for relaxation. There are many parties and lots of friends coming and going. All summer long the Rhoodmen enjoy themselves.

As the days start to get shorter preparations are made for the coming of winter.

One of the early autumn tasks is the harvesting of the crop of koko nuts which can be found in the warmer parts of Rhoodland, and which are valued for their milk.

They are taken high into the hills and laid out in careful stacks in the coolest spots.

comes swiftly to Rhoodland
and the earth turns to white iron.

When the temperature falls below freezing, the koko nuts are picked up and shaken in order to form ice cream, a favoured treat in Rhoodland.

When the Rhoodmen estimate that the ice-cream is made, they take the koko nuts into deep caves and insulate them with bundles of straw, so that the ice-cream will stay frozen long into the next year.

As the houseboats become icebound some Rhoodmen return to their toadstool homes for the winter. Other's however, stay on and lay in stores aboard their boats.

With the coming of winter it is a busy time for the Rhoodmen. Used equipment is repaired, old skills are practiced and new inventions designed.

Folk dancing is performed...

...and rhoodic arm wrestling helps to keep the Rhoodman fit during their confinement.

Lectures are given on new designs...

Even the Rhood boys take part.

All in all a great deal of
creative thinking goes on!

Flying
has fascinated Rhoodmen for generations...

...but it was the

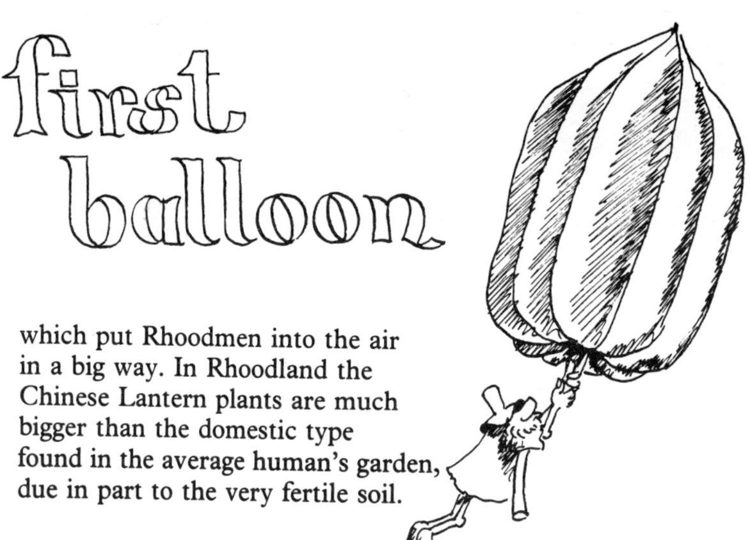

which put Rhoodmen into the air in a big way. In Rhoodland the Chinese Lantern plants are much bigger than the domestic type found in the average human's garden, due in part to the very fertile soil.

Rhoofus tells us that it was he who first accidentally discovered the Chinese Lantern balloon in the following way.

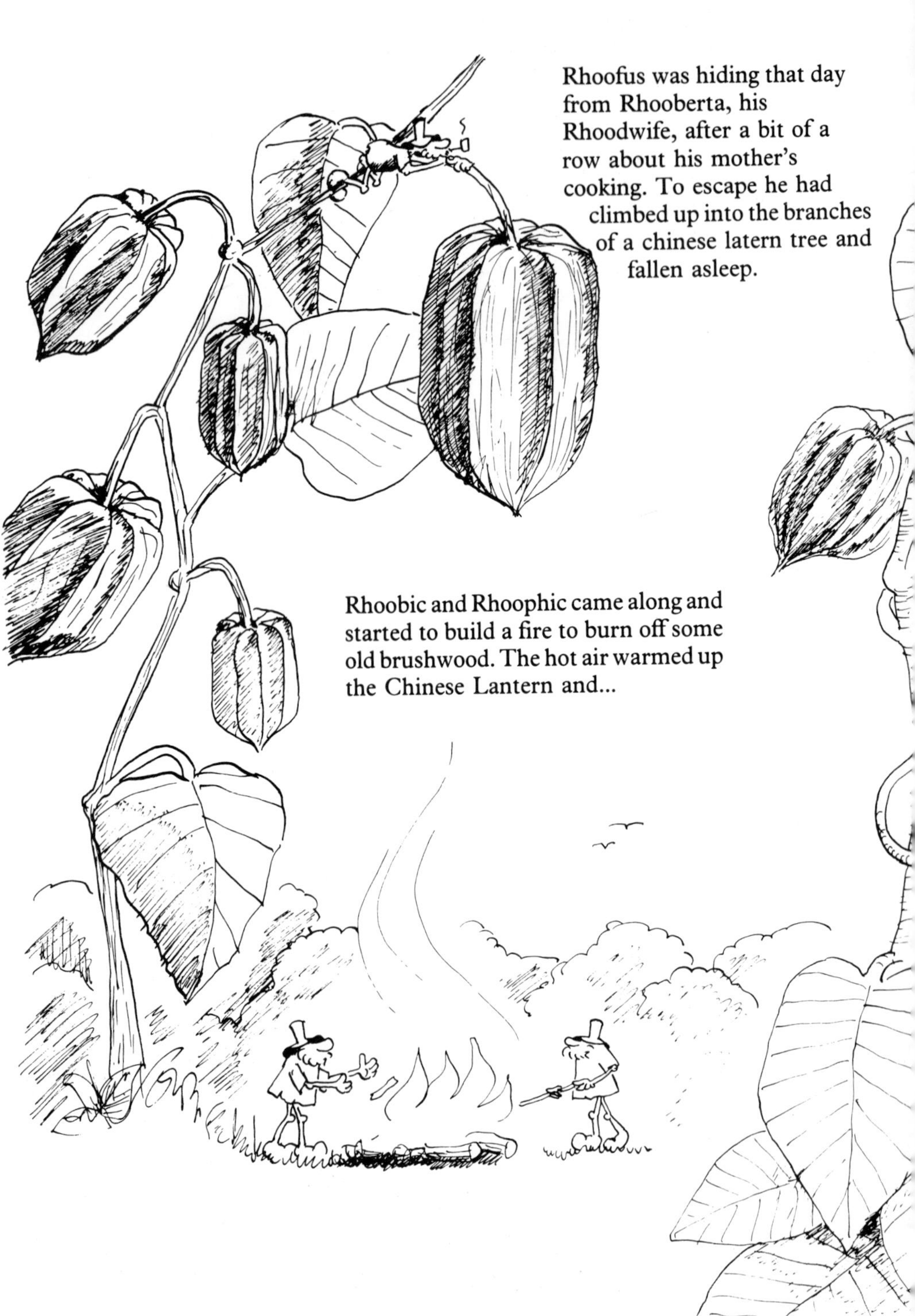

Rhoofus was hiding that day from Rhooberta, his Rhoodwife, after a bit of a row about his mother's cooking. To escape he had climbed up into the branches of a chinese latern tree and fallen asleep.

Rhoobic and Rhoophic came along and started to build a fire to burn off some old brushwood. The hot air warmed up the Chinese Lantern and...

Rhoofus' nose started to tickle with the smoke. The next thing...

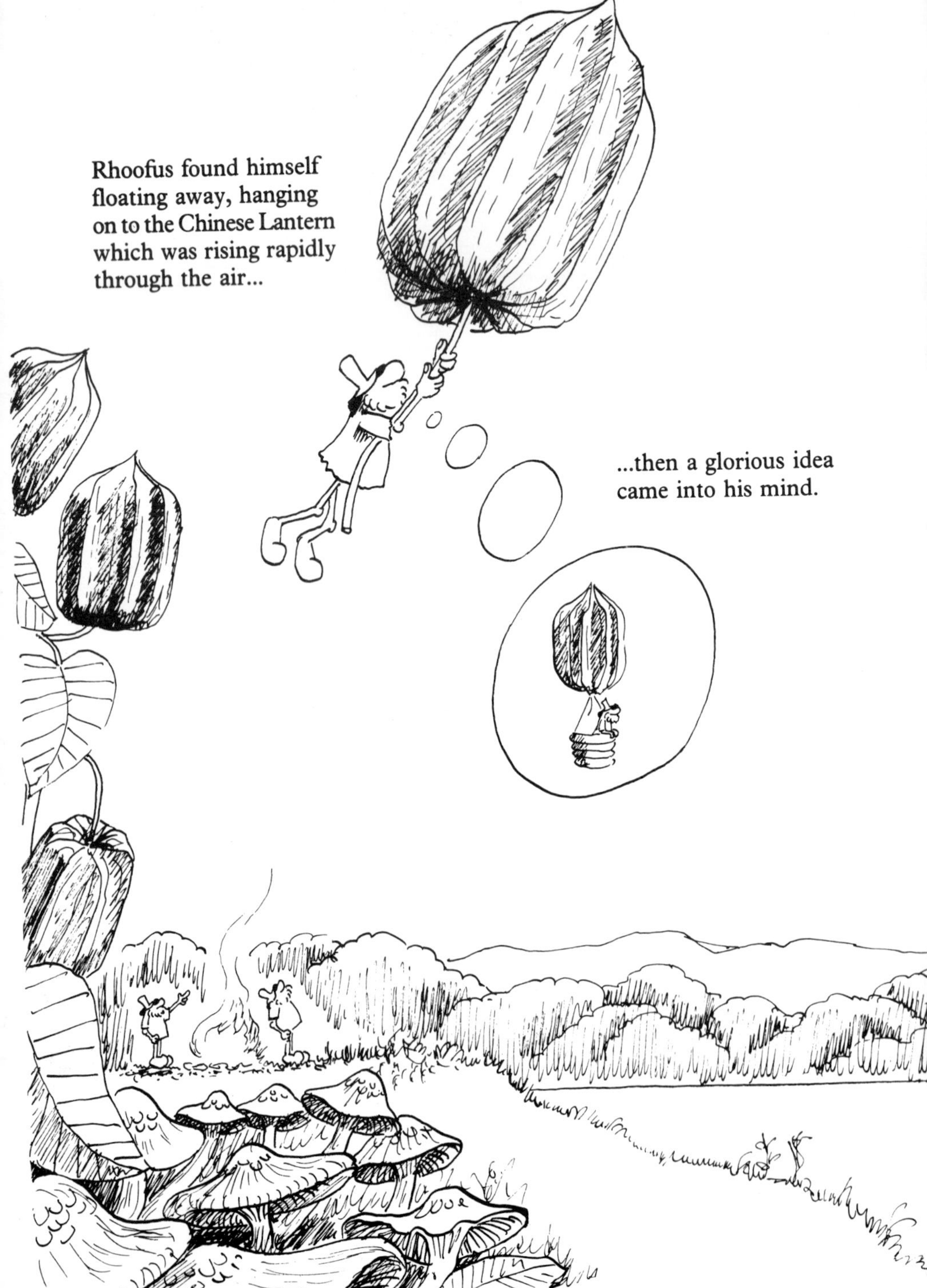
Rhoofus found himself floating away, hanging on to the Chinese Lantern which was rising rapidly through the air...
...then a glorious idea came into his mind.

Impulsively he reached for his
drawing stick and paper not
thinking...
...of the inevitable consequences

Undeterred by his wetting he set to work, making first a basket...

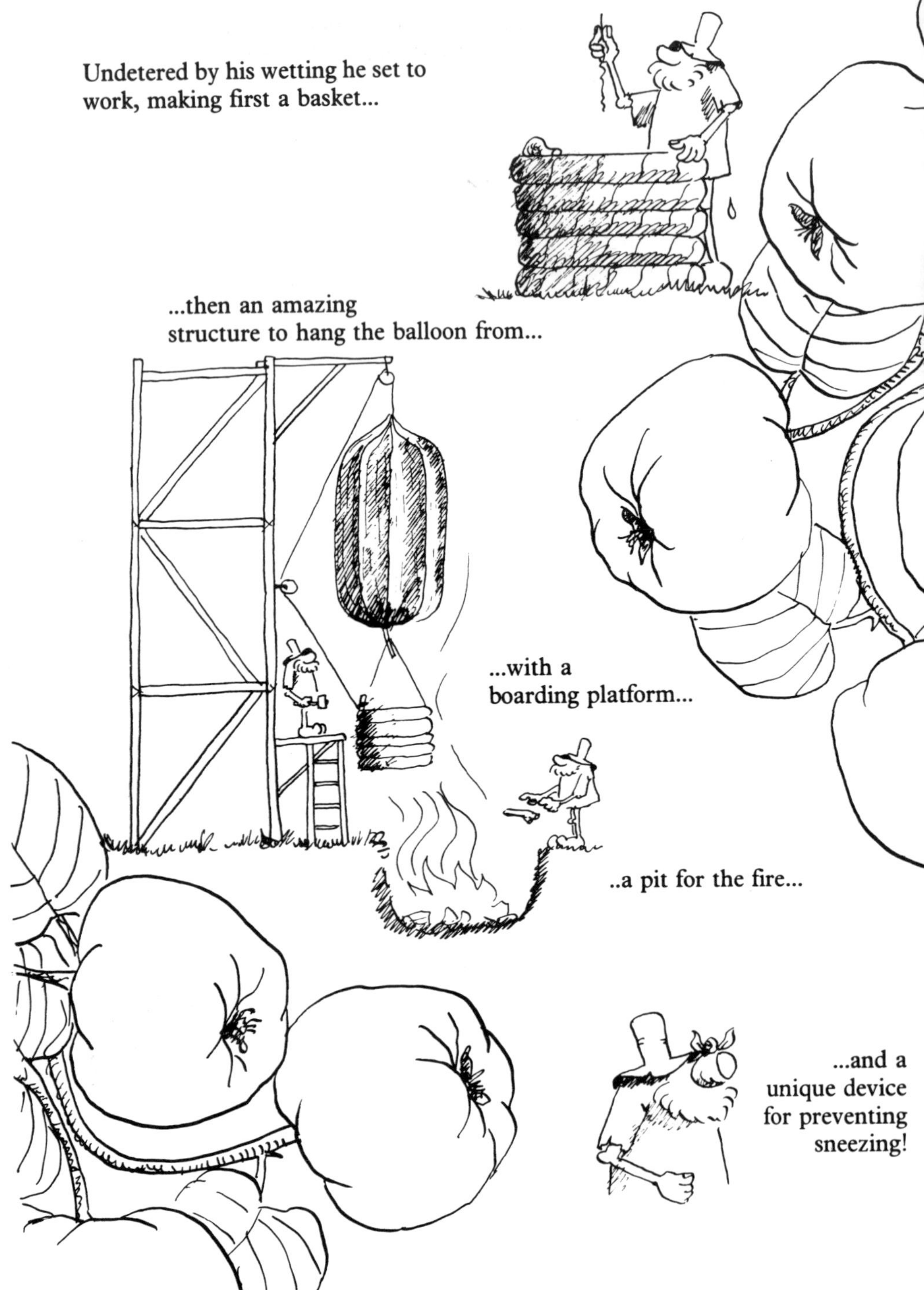

...then an amazing structure to hang the balloon from...

...with a boarding platform...

..a pit for the fire...

...and a unique device for preventing sneezing!

On the day, the balloon worked perfectly. Rhoofus was carried far out over the lake, with a splendid view of Rhoodland...

...and the other Rhoodmen said

So Rhoofus built many more...

...and everyone went for a ride.

Games

On Midsummer Day the Rhoodmen play the traditional game of Running Round the Rhoodstone, the origins of which are steeped in the mists of Time. It is a game of endurance and some say that it evolved from early contests of strength to keep up their hunting skills. A great deal of training goes into it, since much honour and prestige hangs on the result.

The game is played between two teams, nine men in each. The 'batting' team puts in its first player, who starts from half way round the Great Rhood Stone. The fielding team also put in their man, who starts from the other side. On the command go they both run off in a clockwise direction, trying to catch the other player and singing the Ragged Rhoodman ditty. Every time a player passes the table he has to drink a flagon of beer before running on. When one player catches the other the innings is over and the catcher's team is awarded one point. At the end of the match the team with the most points is declared the winner and allowed to use the toilet first!

Rhoofus claims to be the first to discover the delights of Rhoodland beer. By now, dear reader, you may have got the idea that Rhoofus' main fault is his incurable lack of modesty. Be that as it may, it all seems to have come about as a result of a little tiff with the wife, so maybe domestic crisis have their uses.

He had been, it seems, away from home that day looking for some hazel nuts for the pot. Rhooberta was making a nut casserole as all Rhoodmen love their nuts.

So leaving Rhooberta to heat the water he wandered off. It was a warm afternoon. The birds sang and the crickets chirped. It was one of those lazy summer days which Rhoodland seems to make a speciality of. Rhoofus, after a tiring and fruitless search sat down in the sun by a rock.

He layed down.
Just for a few moments.
Honestly!

Six hours later, with the sun setting behind the trees he woke with a start.

Then he remembered Rhooberta... and the nuts. Or rather, lack of nuts.

Jumping to his feet he grabbed the nearest plants which looked vaguely edible and ran off home to Rhooberta, who was waiting in the gathering gloom of the evening.
oof!
His welcome was less than ecstatic!
barley
Bash! went the rolling pin.
Crash: went the pan down into the fire. Out went the fire and in went the barley (for that was what he had found).
to mother

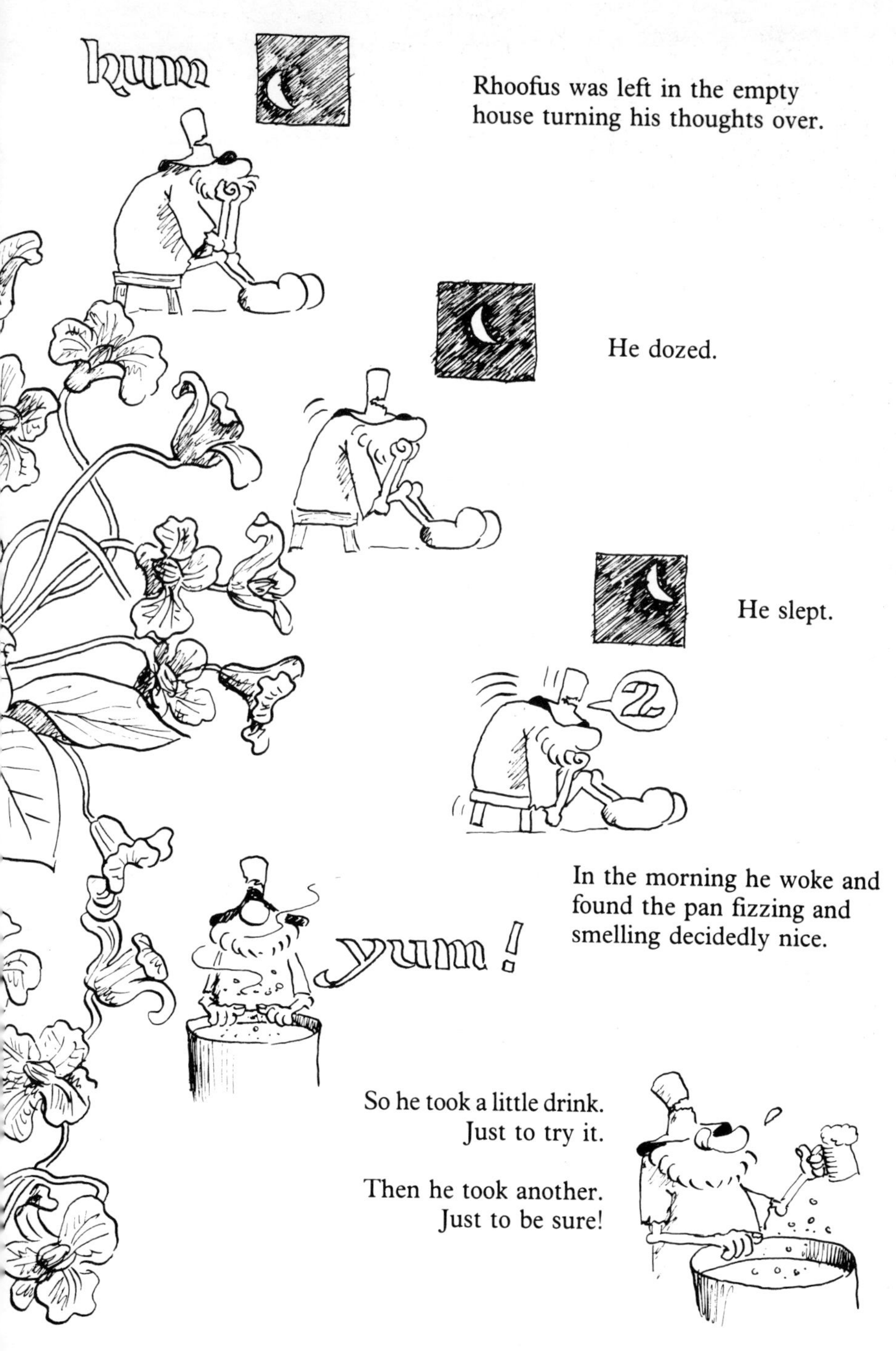

Rhoofus was left in the empty house turning his thoughts over.

He dozed.

He slept.

In the morning he woke and found the pan fizzing and smelling decidedly nice.

So he took a little drink.
Just to try it.

Then he took another.
Just to be sure!

by lunchtime he was unashamedly

drunk!

because the barley had 'mashed' in the cooling water to form the wort which had fermented with wild yeast to form beer!

Other Rhoodmen heard his revelling and came over. They, too, drank the beautiful amber liquid. The result can be imagined!

By the end of the day they were all snoring peacefully in the long grass.

And that, claims Rhoofus, is how he discovered beer. Some say that Rhooberta invented hangovers in revenge, though this has never been proved.

Z
the end